EXODUS

THE LORD AND HIS PILGRIMS

10 Publishing
a division of 10 of those.com

First published in Great Britain in 2016

British Library Cataloguing in Publication Data

A record for this book is available from the British Library

ISBN: 978-1-910587-62-1
Designed by Diane Warnes
Printed in the UK

10Publishing, a division of 10ofthose.com
Unit C, Tomlinson Road, Leyland, PR25 2DY, England
Email: info@10ofthose.com
Website: www.10ofthose.com

Alec Motyer

40 UNDATED DEVOTIONS THROUGH THE BOOK OF EXODUS

INTRODUCTION

The simplest way to look at the book of Exodus is to see it in four sections:

1. A slave people under sentence of death (1:1 - 5:21). The scene is set in chapter 1 where the current Pharaoh or king of Egypt determines on a genocidal policy. In chapter 2 Moses is born, but fails in his attempt to liberate his people. He flees to Midian, but in chapters 3–4 is called by God to return and bring Israel out of Egypt. His first encounter with Pharaoh, in chapter 5, is a failure.

2. The Lord's great work of liberation and redemption (5:22 - 12:51). In 5:22 - 7:7 Moses, together with Aaron, is restored to the task of delivering Israel. The plagues (7:8 - 11:10) are Pharaoh's period of probation, giving him every opportunity to obey the Lord's word and release the people. The final plague achieves this purpose (11:1–9). In chapter 12 the Passover sacrifice of a lamb shelters the Israelites on the night the Lord comes himself in judgment and they leave Egypt as the Lord's redeemed people.

3. The Journey to Sinai: Israel walks with God and learns his requirements (13:1 - 24:18). The Lord cares for his people as they travel from Egypt to Sinai (13:1 - 19:25). At Sinai they learn his law and promise obedience (20:1 - 24:18).

4. A slave people who built cities for Pharaoh (1:11) provide a tabernacle for the Lord himself to live among them (25:1 - 40:38). Moses is given the blueprint (25:1 - 31:18). In spite of the great sin of the golden calf (chapters 32–33), the covenant is renewed (chapter 34) and the building goes ahead. All its various parts are assembled (35:1 - 39:43) and finally erected (40:1–28).

Within the book of Exodus as a whole, two important points need to be established:

1. The story of the Exodus is a visual aid teaching about law and grace. An Israelite of Moses' day would have given much the same testimony as you or I. He would have said, 'I was a slave under a king determined to put me to death. Moses said: take a lamb and shelter under its blood. I did so, and the Lord saved me.' In other words, the Exodus is a story of saving grace. It is about not my worthiness but God's goodness; it is due to nothing that I did, but what he provided in the blood of the lamb. This is what the Old Testament calls 'redemption'. What happened next? They set out for the Promised Land, following the cloudy–fiery pillar (13:21–22), and in the first instance the pillar led them not to Canaan but to Mount Sinai, where the Lord gave them his Law (chapters 19–20). God's law, in the Bible, is not a ladder we try to climb to get into God's good books; it is a way of life the Lord gives to his redeemed people because they are already in his good books through his work of redemption. Grace always comes first; law follows, so that we who have been redeemed know how to live so as to delight our Redeemer.

2. Moses dominates the story. From start to finish Exodus is about Moses. Born under a special providential protection of God, disciplined in Midian to learn to shepherd another man's sheep (3:1; cf. Ps. 77:20) and sent back as the liberator, Moses was Israel's leader right through the wilderness to the border of the Promised Land. He is central to the whole story and much of it concerns what took place privately between him and God, so that he is the only source of the information. Unbroken tradition summarises all this by calling Exodus 'the second book of Moses', and there is no reason to question that attribution. All known leaders in antiquity kept daily written records of their leadership; Moses was no different.

DAY 1

READ Exodus 1:1–22

Whose word will win?

God keeps his promises – and God's promise always come under threat. At first sight verses 1–7 say nothing that is not already in Genesis 46:1–27 – Israel's arrival in Egypt; the tribes identified; and God's reassurances to Jacob on facing such a risky move. But just comparing verse 7 with Genesis 46:3 will do here for our purposes: *when God makes a promise, he keeps it!* Did Israel in Egypt notice that this promise was being kept? Maybe not. Were they too preoccupied with the harshness of life to take into account what Pharaoh had noticed (Ex. 1:9) – the huge multiplication of the immigrant community? If so, they deprived themselves of the consolation of seeing the faithfulness of their God. A promise had been made and that promise was being magnificently kept. This truth – that God always keeps his promises – is actually a fair summary of the whole book of Exodus, but it is strikingly seen in the first chapter.

But hot on the heels of this great truth comes its biblical counterpart: *there is no such thing as an unchallenged word of God.* When the word comes, counterattack is immediate (Mark 4:15) and tribulation looms (Mark 4:17). Egypt is a case in point. Pharaoh saw increasing numbers, sensed increasing danger (Ex: 1:10), and mounted a considered response. First, we read of 'burdens', affliction and taskmasters who 'ruthlessly' make them work (vv. 11–14, ESV). As the developing story indicates, this continues (see 5:5ff.) even when it is seen not to work (1:12). Secondly, there comes the secret attempt to conscript the midwives (vv. 15–21). Their motive for non-cooperation is spiritual (v. 17), but we can see that God was standing by his word. Finally, Pharaoh resorts to a public policy of genocide (v. 22), and the chapter ends with this question hanging in the air: will the enemy succeed at long last?

No, the enemy will not succeed, but, simply staying with Exodus 1, we see first that the purposes of God cannot be halted (v. 12), and secondly, as Isaiah 59:19 puts it, 'When the enemy comes in like a flood, the Spirit of the LORD will lift up a standard against him' (cf. Ex. 1:17).

REFLECTION

Trials are not 'strange' (1 Pet. 4:12); they are God's intended way of spiritual progress (Jas. 1:2–4); and they accompany the outpouring of God's love (Rom. 5:3–5).

DAY 2

READ Exodus 2:1–22

God's secret weapon

Aslan, the Great Lion of Narnia, was right: we are never told what would have happened. There is no point in saying, 'Suppose Moses had got it right ...!' Stop speculating; just look at what is before our eyes: the marvellous working of God.

Out of a genocidal royal house (1:22) emerges a tender-hearted 'daughter' (she is called 'Pharaoh's daughter' five times in 2:5–10, to stress her genetic inheritance) who takes the Hebrew child under her wing (vv. 6, 9–10). The place of death (1:22) becomes the place of life (2:10) – indeed the Nile, designed to drown Israel, in fact drowns Egypt (14:28)! The Hebrew mother, instead of being bereaved, is paid to bring up her child (2:9). Egypt's destroyer is nourished in Egypt's royal family (v. 10; cf. Acts 7:21–22). Pharaoh's daughter does not know that her walk by the river is divinely 'managed' as to time and place; nor does Miriam know that her careful choice of a place where the baby's 'ark' (as the NKJV puts it) will be held by rushes and not carried away by the current is hand-picked by God! Pharaoh's daughter's unthinking walk and the family's plan of care are alike in *his* hand.

But it is a tense moment when Pharaoh's daughter opens the 'ark'. The Hebrew says, 'When she saw him – the child –...' She takes note of his masculinity; he is a child sentenced to death. Surely her lineage would cause her to promptly chuck the baby in the river? But no. Divine sovereignty destined this child not for the river but for the palace! How very marvellous is the providential working of God! Humanly speaking we would say Moses promptly got it all wrong and set God's programme back by forty years (vv. 11–15; Acts 7:30), but God's sovereign providence is more wonderful than that: what we think of as his forward planning has taken account of our errors. See how God had a home waiting for Moses in Midian (vv. 16–21) – a wife, family, and a flock (3:1) – so that he could learn to be the shepherd God's people would need (Ps. 77:20).

REFLECTION

Divine sovereignty is at work in a world seemingly governed by chance (Prov. 16:33). Here we see the wonderful 'blending' of divine sovereignty and human responsibility (Prov. 16:9; Acts 2:23).

READ Exodus 2:23 – 3:10

The new start

Nothing happens on earth until decisions are made in heaven. Israel's situation is dire, but the vital question is what does God intend to do about it (2:23–25)? Moses is God's chosen agent but the priority for him is not action (cf. 2:11–14!) but to meet and know God (3:1–6), who is:

- The prayer-answering God. There are three verbs in 2:23: to 'groan' and to 'cry out' (literally, 'scream') express need; the third, 'to cry for help' (NIV), is prayer – and that brings the vital change.
- The caring, promise-keeping God. In verses 24–25, there are four verbs of God identifying with his people: he 'heard ... remembered ... looked upon ... was concerned' (NIV; literally, 'knew'). The Lord's 'covenant' is his promise to take and keep his people (cf. Gen. 6:18 – literally, 'I will implement ...'; 46:4).
- The living God (3:2), revealed in a self-perpetuating flame that needs no fuel to feed on. He is, therefore, a God independently free to do what he wills; he needs nothing outside himself and is utterly sufficient.
- The holy God (v. 5). On the one hand, God is inapproachable; on the other, he makes it easy for those who dare not approach him to come near (Heb. 10:22; 1 Pet. 3:18).
- The God of the past (Ex. 3:6), the present (v. 7) and the future (v. 8). He is the God who sovereignly conscripts and commands his chosen agents (vv. 9–10).

If you sense that the Lord's dealings with Moses were more than a bit peremptory, you are right! From God's opening words, 'Moses, Moses!' (v. 4), to his final 'Come now' (v. 10), Moses is given no room for manoeuvre. We forget this to our detriment. We come into the presence of God through the unobtrusive mediation of Jesus. We come through the forgiving Mediator to the forgiving Father. Grace provides the way in; love overshadows us. His divine voice says, 'Come in, and welcome'; but we enter the presence of the awesomely holy One; we stand before the eternal Majesty; we come into the place of authority, conscription and direction. The only proper reply is, 'Speak, LORD, for Your servant hears' (1 Sam. 3:9).

REFLECTION

Think about the greatness of God. Psalm 86:8–13 will give your thoughts a framework. Use verse 10 as a repeated cry of praise.

DAY 4

READ Exodus 3:11–22

Knowing God

From 3:11 – 4:17 Moses raises a series of objections to the Lord's call, starting with his sense of inadequacy: 'Who am I ...?' (3:11). The Lord in effect replies to this: 'What matters is who am I!' Christians should never pray to lose their sense of inadequacy but rather to fill their inadequacy with the adequacy of the God who promises to be with them (v. 12). This is, in fact, the significance of the puzzling and enigmatic name the Lord gives himself: 'I AM WHO I AM' (v. 14). As things work out in Exodus we could spell out the name like this: 'I alone know who I am. You are dependent on what I reveal to you. In every situation I will show you that I am what you need.' And indeed so it was. They needed a deliverer (from Egyptian power) and a redeemer to bring them to God: The Lord revealed himself as Deliverer and Redeemer (6:6–7). Indeed, this became, throughout the Old Testament, the basic definition of 'I AM WHO I AM' – the God who overthrows his foes and saves his people.

It remains a bit of a mystery why Moses thinks people will ask him the name of the God he has met (v. 13). Some suggest that maybe asking for the name is equivalent to asking, 'What revelation of God do you bring?' This seems to me a bit roundabout, and I wonder if, through all their Egyptian years, the Hebrews had kept secret their God's name and, at the crucial moment, they could use it as a test: if Moses really had met the God of their fathers (v. 15), he would be 'in' on the secret, and knowing the name would authenticate his mission. This is in line with Jesus' command, 'Take heed what you hear' (Mark 4:24), and John's injunction to 'not believe every spirit, but test the spirits, whether they are of God' (1 John 4:1) because false prophets abound. It means subjecting everything to the test of Scripture: 'What is written in the law? What is your reading of it?' (Luke 10:26).

REFLECTION

Jesus also said, 'Therefore take heed how you hear' (Luke 8:18). Bible reading has got to be more than moving the bookmark on a page.

READ Exodus 4:1–28

Provision and demand

Persistently, Moses goes on finding excuses for not fulfilling his God-given role – he raises first his lack of persuasive authority (v. 1) and then that he is without the gift of speech needed for the task (v. 10). Finally he pleads to God: 'please send someone else' (v. 13, NIV). In response, the Lord goes on countering Moses' excuses. We must not overlook the marvel of divine patience. Where Moses feels impotent, the Lord imparts power (vv. 2–9). The serpent was part of Egypt's imperial crown; the Nile its semi-divine river. God enables Moses to become master of both – and deals with Moses' own impurities too (vv. 6–7). What are the tongue's inadequacies compared with the promised power of the tongue's Creator (v. 12). The 'I AM' is sufficient and will reveal himself so.

But why after all that patience should the Lord then seek to kill Moses (vv. 24–26)? We must note the following:

- The underlying issue was that Moses' son had not been circumcised, and as soon as Zipporah, Moses' wife, put this right, the crisis was over (v. 25).
- Not only did Zipporah somehow realise this but she also acted on behalf of the immobilised Moses (v. 25).
- Touching Moses with the blood (v. 25; literally, 'made it touch his feet') identified him with what she had done, and her words mean, 'Instead of our marriage ending, the blood has made you my bridegroom all over again.'

It is, without doubt, a strange and unexpected incident, but it carries a very important message: those who go about the Lord's business must be meticulous in their obedience. Having settled in a foreign land, was Moses disinclined to go against surrounding social norms? Maybe circumcision didn't matter all that much? But it did! The messengers of the covenant of God must be the first to keep his covenant (Gen. 17:9–14). Those who are the Lord's vessels must give priority to holiness (Is. 52:11). Read the requirements for being 'overseers' in the church (1 Tim. 3:1–7; Tit. 1:7–9) – they are very ordinary virtues, aren't they? Would not every Christian wish to be like that? Yes, and that is exactly the point: those 'up front' must be 'exhibit A' of what it is like to be a Christian!

REFLECTION

Think about verse 27. The Lord is present in every place; every heart and mind in under his sway; he calls his agents but remains in control.

DAY 6

READ Exodus 4:29 – 5:21

Why don't you do what you're told?

I think we would have to say that initial success (4:29–31) goes to Moses' head. He had had a sharp experience, in 2:12–22, that 'the wrath of man does not produce the righteousness of God' (Jas. 1:20), but obviously the lesson has not quite gone home. He certainly acts as if he thinks he is on a roll, bouncing into Pharaoh's presence with strident demands (Ex. 5:1)! This is not what he was told to do (3:18). If we compare 3:12 with 5:1–2 we see it is all a multiple error: the wrong delegation (Moses and Aaron, 5:1, not Moses and the elders, as specified in 3:18); the wrong approach (an authoritarian 'Thus says the LORD God of Israel ...', v. 1); the wrong terminology ('Israel' instead of 'the Hebrews', which would have been familiar to Pharaoh); the wrong request (liberation instead of three-day permission); and a non-negotiable demand ('Let ... go'), rather than a negotiating position ('three days'). And all this is stated in the name of 'the LORD', Yahweh, a God Pharaoh had never heard of.

Once more, of course, we are not told what would have happened, we only know that, by disobeying, Moses brings his people into unwanted suffering (vv. 6–19), and his mission into disrepute (vv. 20–21). Even the ground Moses had initially gained when the Israelites put their trust in him (4:31) is lost (5:21).

But even when Moses tries to revise his approach (v. 3), he complicates the issue with his own addition: a threat of the sword (5:3) is not mentioned in 3:18 – and there is still the inclusion of the name 'the LORD'. Probably Pharaoh's question 'Who is the LORD' (5:2) was a genuine request for information, not an arrogant repudiation.

Now we need to notice that nothing Moses said to Pharaoh was untrue, but, in the strictest sense, first, the word of God was set aside (v. 1), and secondly, an addition from human logic and wisdom was given (v. 3). 'Stewards' are required to be faithful (1 Cor. 4:2), not inventive; 'ambassadors' are required to speak as if their overlord was himself speaking (2 Cor. 5:20), not to add their own 'spin'; 'prophets' throughout the Old Testament characteristically say, 'Thus says the Lord', meaning 'this is what the Lord has said'. How crucially important then, for us, is scriptural exactitude (1 Cor. 4:6)!

REFLECTION

Disobedience to God's word all started in Eden. When Adam and Eve added to what God had said about safeguarding the tree, they opened a door for Satan (Gen. 3:3).

The great NOW

The Bible does not sweep our problems under the carpet as insignificant. Today's passage begins and ends by noting Moses' despondency and inadequacy (5:22–23; 6:9–12), and it is to this the Lord gives his full attention (6:1–8). The remedy is effectively: 'look away from yourself and fill your eyes with me.' There are two aspects to this:

1. They had long known the name 'the Lord' (see Gen. 4:26), but until now they did not know exactly what the name signified (Ex. 6:2–3 literally reads, 'as regards my name, Yahweh, I did not make myself known to them.'). The title 'God Almighty' (*El Shaddai*) carried a wonderful truth as the context to the references shows: he is the God who is at his strongest when people are at their weakest (Gen. 17:1; 28:3; 35:11; 43:14; 48:3; 49:25). How could the childless Abram become a father? How would the solitary Jacob face an uncertain future? How would Joseph's brothers fare with the despotic, unpredictable ruler of Egypt? Indeed how would Joseph himself survive when 'under the cosh' of Pharaoh? They all needed an all-powerful God.

2. The way 'covenant' links Exodus 6:4–5 means that all the virtues of *El Shaddai*, the covenant God, are still available for crushed Israel and despondent Moses. But there is more: 'the LORD' (vv. 6–7) is specifically the God of deliverance (from Egypt) and redemption (as my people). Exodus chapters 6–12 trace both these exercises: the power that shatters the power of the enemy, and the blood that brings them home safely to God.

Redemption (v. 6) is one of the great words of the Bible. So what does it mean? The Hebrew word in question is *goel*, the next-of-kin whose right it is to take on himself whatever burden his nearest kinsman is carrying. Remember Boaz, in the book of Ruth? He could not act to lift Naomi and Ruth out of poverty and Ruth out of childless widowhood unless he was the next-of-kin (Ruth 3:12), but when the actual next-of-kin stepped back (4:6), this position devolved on Boaz who accepted it with alacrity (4:9–10, 13). Yahweh is our divine Next-of-kin, taking our burdens as if his own, paying our debt and bearing our sin: he is our *Goel*.

REFLECTION

When the New Testament uses the title 'Lord' of Jesus, it intends us to identify him with the redeemer God the Old Testament reveals (Gal. 3:13; Phil. 2:11; Col. 2:6; Rev. 5:9).

DAY 8

READ Exodus 6:28 – 7:24

Obedience: a lesson learnt

We haven't read 6:13–27 but these verses have a point to make. Their testimony is that Moses and Aaron are the same frail human clay they have always been; the revelation of Yahweh has given them a fresh awareness of him but left them unchanged. This is exactly the point. Amid all our human frailty we face life with our eyes on him, looking to him, expecting from him and relying on him. Hence we read the key verse (7:6) which will dominate the rest of the Exodus story: precise, detailed obedience.

Moses is to do what Yahweh says and leave the outcome to him. This comprises doing something silly, like throwing a rod on the ground (v. 9); something seemingly pointless like killing a lamb (12:6); and something involving power beyond the human – calling for darkness (10:21). Yet Moses must just do what Yahweh says and leave the outcome to him – that's how Israel escaped Egypt's power and threat. It is what is called 'the obedience of faith' – whereas humanity says, 'I can't, so I won't', faith says, 'I can't, but *he* can, so I will.' This was the Lord's promise to Moses: 'I have made you as God to Pharaoh' (7:1). Though Pharaoh himself is 'god', Moses goes to him with the promise of equal stature!

In 7:14 the narrative of the plagues begins to be carefully told: the first two dominate the 'godlike' Nile; three and four are united in kind; five and six are skin eruptions respectively on animals and humans; seven and eight destroy crops; and nine and ten, symbolically and then actually, express wrath against sin. Plagues 1, 4, and 7 begin at the river; 2, 5 and 8 begin in the palace; 3, 6 and 9 are unannounced. It may be that some of the plagues can be reasonably traced to 'natural causes' but they are all the judgmental acts of God designed to give Pharaoh and Egypt a prolonged period of probation. Each trial is a test of obedience and grace, holding back the ultimate judgment in hope of its being rendered unnecessary by repentance.

REFLECTION

According to James, we are placed no differently from Pharaoh. The tests of life are designed to implement spiritual progress (Jas. 1:2–4, 12–18).

DAY 9

READ Exodus 8:1–19

Evidence but no eyes

In ancient Egyptian theology, the creator 'god', Khnum, took a wife, a 'goddess', who had a frog's head! What he created, she endowed with life. The second plague is a direct challenge to this belief. The 'divine' Nile, itself the basis of Egypt's life, becomes the source of death (v. 3). Then the limitations of false religion are exposed: the magicians can replicate this plague but they cannot stem or remedy it (v. 7). Pharaoh, who did not know 'the LORD' (5:2) is obliged to recognise Yahweh and asks Moses to pray to him that the frogs are taken away (8:8). Moses states that this will happen as final evidence that there is no God like Yahweh (v. 10). Thus the plague ends, yet not with the frogs hopping back into the Nile (cf. 10:19) but in their death. Previously the elders had complained Moses made them stink (5:21) but now it is Egypt that stinks (v. 14).

Like all the plagues, the plague of frogs can be seen as a hurtful exercise of power. Really, though, it is a convincing demonstration of who the true God is, and of his mercy in answer to prayer. Pharaoh's heart hardening (v. 15) is a wilful resistance to this truth (cf. Rom. 1:20–24, 28).

The third plague (vv. 16–19), like the sixth (9:8–12) and the ninth (10:21–29), comes unannounced to Pharaoh, and is a direct response to his heart hardening (8:15; 9:7; 10:20). The Lord throws down a direct challenge: 'My people ... serve Me' (8:1). Pharaoh is unwilling to yield dominance. The combat of the two begun, the third plague therefore is a direct warning to Pharaoh to submit and obey.

It is not certain quite what the third plague was. The word has been translated gnats, lice, mosquitoes, maggots and sand flies. Certainly the unpleasantness is gruesome to imagine. This plague also marks the limit of the magicians' powers: this time, still unable to limit or remedy it, they cannot even replicate it, and so they acknowledge that they are faced by a superior power (v. 19). But their readiness to cry 'enough' collides with the increasingly impervious heart of their king (v. 19). Wrong choices do that: they bring the human will closer and closer to the point of no return where the power of choice itself has died.

REFLECTION

Ponder the words of this hymn: 'Take my will, and make it thine; it shall be no longer mine. Take my heart, it is thine own; it shall be thy royal throne.' [1]

DAY 10

READ Exodus 8:20 – 9:12

Pharaoh's negotiating positions

This passage details the fourth, fifth and sixth plagues. Our focus today, though, is Pharaoh: he still has enough liberty of movement left to try negotiating a compromise with Moses. Without any help from me, you will recognise how up-to-date his compromise suggestions and their temptations are! He proposes in turn:

1. Why not make your Yahweh one of the gods of Egypt (8:25)? In other words Pharaoh is saying, 'There's no need to be so standoffish! Settle down and join in! We prefer Ra and Knum; you prefer Yahweh. Let's learn from each other and be good neighbours!' 'No,' says Moses in effect, 'your religion cannot accommodate ours (v. 26); our God has his unique requirements (v. 27). We are bound by what he chooses to tell us: ours is a revealed religion.'

2. If you must be different, try not to be as different as all that: stay close (v. 28), that is, stay in the world even if you're not of it. Yet this is not God's way – he sets his people apart (8:22); he makes a total separation (9:4, cf. v. 26). That is non-negotiable. Likewise we don't seek to be different; we just are! (John 15:19).

3. From Moses' reply (Ex. 8:10–11) we can infer a suggestion that perhaps children remain in Egypt and only adults go. If we thus understand the emphasis in his words, then Pharaoh is suggesting that it would be a good thing to keep a foot in both camps: why force your convictions on your children; let them grow up and make up their own minds! To this Moses replies with a stark refusal, but behind it lies God's insistence that our children are within his covenant (Gen. 17:12–13); the gathered people has an essential family component.

4. Alter the nature of your Israelite religion (Ex. 10:24). Pharaoh yields regarding allowing women and children to go but tries to impose an embargo on flocks and herds.

Moses is inflexible in facing and outfacing Pharaoh, yet he is not unyielding. When Pharaoh asks for respite (8:28), Moses very likely realises it is insincere, but he meets Pharaoh's request: this too is a lesson to learn.

REFLECTION

Remember these four points on which compromise is forbidden: the basis of religion is in revelation; we are a distinctive people; we must educate and include our children in our devotions; and sacrifice is at the heart of worship.

Pharaoh's heart

Pharaoh's heart has been part of the Exodus storyline so far (4:21; 7:3, 13, 14, 23; 8:15, 19, 32; 9:7, 12), and, at first sight, it is a puzzle how on one hand the Lord hardened his heart, and on the other blamed him for having a hard heart! It seems impossibly unjust, and we need to think carefully about it. Now, in fact, Exodus here, while recounting the seventh plague, says three distinct things about Pharaoh's heart. They are all true and must all be kept in mind, and are all found in 9:34–10:1: he 'hardened his heart', together with his officials (9:34), his heart became hardened (v. 35, literally) and God proclaimed, 'I have hardened his heart' (10:1).

So first, Pharaoh 'hardened his heart' (9:34; cf. 8:15; see 7:22). Pharaoh set himself to disobey: his heart-hardening was his own deliberate, wilful refusal of God's word. As a result of this decision, secondly, his heart was hardened (v. 35). That's what always happens: a decision made becomes a predisposition to go that way again. This is something we all know about: it is called 'habit-forming' – and sadly it can most easily be illustrated in the case of bad habits. A first experience proves attractive, and makes another try more likely and easier to submit to. First and second combine forces to make a third, and then a fourth easier still – until, somewhere along this line of trial and temptation, we are 'hooked'; a point of no return has been reached. We can never see that point coming; we only know it by hindsight. Yet the all-righteous God knows it in advance. It is his decision: we have toyed with sin long enough; now we must pay the penalty. So it was for Pharaoh when Moses confronted him. We are not told Pharaoh's prehistory; we are only informed that Moses' call for obedience was his point of no return; one more refusal to go God's way would seal his fate by the moment of irreversible heart-hardening. God hardened his heart. The act had become a habit; the habit a divine judgment. That is what we see thirdly in 10:1.

REFLECTION

Think about the words of this hymn: 'Prone to wander, Lord, I feel it, prone to leave the God I love; here's my heart, O take and seal it, seal it for thy courts above.' [2]

Power, patience and finality

The sequence of the plagues nears its end with a demonstration of absolute power over all the power of the enemy – a needed and salutary truth for today surely! Egypt had a 'god' for every eventuality. For example, Senehem was invoked to protect the land from the ravages of pests. Until, of course, Yahweh, without a 'by your leave', wills the locusts to fill the land in the eighth plague. He sends them (v. 4), and Pharaoh recognises that Yahweh alone can remove them (v. 17). Things go even a step higher. The Egyptian god Amon-Ra – their chief deity, the personification of the sun and their ruler of the sequence of day and night – is first blotted out by Yahweh's locusts (v. 15), then his characteristic activity as the light-bringer is annulled by Yahweh's darkness in the ninth plague (vv. 21–22).

Whether the object of worship concerned is a lesser object of worship (Senehem) or the greatest (Amon-Ra) is of no significance. The Lord on high is mightier (Ps. 93:3–4). But his is always a power working by mercy, like an old prayer says: 'he declares his almighty power most chiefly by showing mercy and pity'. We could easily overlook the 'for' (literally, 'because') in verse 1 – God in reality is saying, 'Tell Pharaoh the truth *because* I have hardened his heart!' The only way to break through the hard heart is the declaration of the truth, and right to the end the Lord is still pleading with Pharaoh! These two great truths are not at odds, nor are they competitors for attention. They are both always present and active. But while power knows no end, patience does.

As the parable of the tenants says, 'last of all he sent his son' (Mt. 21:37). At Exodus 9:11 the magicians had had enough; at 10:7 Pharaoh's courtiers threw in their towel; at 10:28 Pharaoh finally breaks off negotiations, siding with his hard heart (v. 27), and receiving from Moses' lips the sentence of death: 'I will never see your face again' (v. 29). But even against the obdurate king, Yahweh's power prevails for Pharaoh is compelled himself to contribute beasts for Yahweh's worship (v. 25).

REFLECTION

We should never cease to pray for those who seem to be the chief public enemies of the Gospel, that they may be saved. God is powerful and just (Ps. 62:11–12).

The ultimate danger; a divine provision

The final plague will be unique in its effectiveness (11:1). It is important to ask and answer the question, 'Why?' The answer (v. 4) is that it is unique in its infliction: the other plagues were imposed, but this time God himself is coming into the heart of Egypt (v. 4). This is the significance of Exodus 11–12. These chapters raise the ultimate question: 'How are we to stand before God when he comes in judgment (12:12); when probation is at an end; when every opportunity of repentance and obedience has been frittered away; and when there is no hiding place?'

Once before, when death threatened, the Lord himself provided a lamb to die instead of Isaac (Gen. 22:7–8, 13). Maybe, therefore, Israel in Egypt does not find it strange that their recourse when death threatens is to 'take ... a lamb' (Ex. 12:3). The same basic principle 'instead of' is to apply, that is, the principle of equivalence or substitution. First, there is a lamb for each household (v. 3); then there is the need to count the number of individuals for whom the lamb will cater (v. 4a); and finally an assessment is made of each person's 'need' (literally, 'eating' or appetite, v. 4b). This, I think, is the reason for choosing the lamb four days ahead of its death (vv. 3, 6), so that the choice might be leisurely, thoughtful and exact. It is also the reason for the burning of any surplus (v. 10). The lamb is for only one thing: to be a substitute for those for whom it is to die, and the burning of what remains makes it exactly so!

We will read tomorrow that there is a death in every house (12:30). In the Egyptian houses it is the dreadful death of the firstborn; in Israel's houses it is the lamb that dies. And it dies not just for Israel's 'firstborn'. No, the Lord had said, 'Israel is My son, My firstborn' (4:22). The lamb is the substitute-equivalent for 'the Israel of God' (Gal. 6:16), the whole people whom the Lord intends to save.

REFLECTION

As one hymn puts it, 'Dear dying Lamb, thy precious blood will never lose its power.'[3] Consider this and also John 1:29–36; 1 Peter 1:18–19 and Revelation 5:9–12; 7:13–17.

READ Exodus 12:1–42

Partakers and pilgrims

'Peace with God' can only come when God is at peace about us – that is, his mind is at peace when he thinks about us; his holiness is at peace when he passes judgment on us; and his heart is at peace when he contemplates welcoming us into his eternity. And all this is comprised in the statement in verse 13: 'when I see the blood, I will pass over you'. God comes in judgment, sees the blood and is at peace 'The blood', of course, stands for the death of the substitute lamb. Under the blood – that is, by the simplicity of entering the blood-marked house – God's firstborn son, the Israel of God, is safe, immune from judgment (vv. 22–23). Likewise, God saved us 'not by works of righteousness which we have done, but according to His mercy' (Tit. 3:5).

We are not astray from the event if we imagine each family's father, who had acted as priest in the death of the lamb and the smearing of its precious blood (Heb. 9:12; 10:19), reverently counting his family into the blood, from the eldest to the infant in its mother's arms, until they are all safe under the blood. It is no wonder, then, that the Lord linked Passover with a weeklong Feast of Unleavened Bread (Ex. 12:14–17). This wonderful festival of the blood could not be allowed to become a quick-passing episode: it was followed by a restful week in which to contemplate its significance annually. Exactly so should we do with Christmas and Easter, and our other great commemorations of the Lord Jesus.

Passover was an end-of-day festival (v. 6), but the participants were required to be dressed for it from early morning with such an active day ahead (v. 11). They wore not the dressing-gown and slippers of those ready for bed, but the girded loins and staff of pilgrimage. Before Passover they could not leave Egypt; after Passover they cannot stay! They eat as those committed to walk with God.

REFLECTION

We are to be people who '... lay aside every weight ... run with endurance ... looking unto Jesus' (Heb. 12:1–2). We too should sing, 'O, pilgrim bound for the heavenly land, never lose sight of Jesus!' [4]

Remember, remember

These verses are the epilogue to the Lord's mighty works of deliverance and redemption, just as 7:8–13 are the prologue. The prologue anticipates the mighty works; the epilogue recapitulates it, and fixes their significance. The regulation in verses 43–51 may well have been occasioned by 12:38: the presence of those who join themselves to Israel in the Exodus but who are not Israelites by birth. Such are (symbolically) brought within the covenant of grace by circumcision (Gen. 17:9–14), and made partakers of Israel's saving experience by admission to Passover.

Genesis 12 moves from the universal scope of Genesis chapters 1–11 (creation, the fall, the flood and the scattering at Babel) to a narrow focus on one man (Abram) and his family – not because the world is forgotten but because it is through Abram the world will be blessed. Just as God's purpose for Abram was worldwide (Gen. 12:3; 22:18), so was his covenant. And this is continued in the Mosaic covenant (Ex. 12:48). The 'son of a stranger or foreigner' (v. 43, literally) who is by nature excluded, can become, by circumcision and Passover, a participating firstborn son (v. 44; cf. 4:22–23). Thus these verses (vv. 43–51) which seem to exclude foreigners are, in fact, an invitation for them to come in and be welcomed.

13:1–2 understandably give a special place to Israel's firstborn (cf. vv. 11–16), who are in a particular sense the beneficiaries of the Passover blood (12:26–27). Very likely the firstborn sons act as Israel's priests (cf. 24:5) until the particular appointment of the tribe of Levi (Num. 3:12–13). The interim institution of the tribe of Levi is necessitated by the great sin of the golden calf (cf. Ex. 32:25–29). Yet the Lord's intention, 'a kingdom of priests' (19:6), is fulfilled in Christ (1 Pet. 2:9).

Verses 3–9 detail the Feast of Unleavened Bread. Here the intention is to replicate the conditions of the Exodus (cf. 12:8, 34, 39) and so keep the great redemption freshly in their memory. Deuteronomy 16:3 calls it 'the bread of affliction', to recall the privations of Egypt.

REFLECTION

Paul treats leaven (yeast) as symbolic of sin in our lives, and calls us, as Christ's Passover people, to purge it out (1 Cor. 5:7–8). This is our equivalent of keeping the Feast.

God's very odd ways

Exodus chapters 13–18 record the initial stage of the great Exodus pilgrimage, from Egypt to Sinai, and contain many suggestive lessons for us as we to encounter the unexpected twists and turns of life's pathway:

1. The unexpected roundabout. The pillar of cloud seems to lead the Israelites in the opposite direction to the way they expect (13:18). But this is purposeful (v. 17): the 'obvious' way is too dangerous, and could prompt backsliding.

2. The need to turn back. Israel is given precise map readings for their retreat (14:2), but look where it brings them: seemingly right into an impossible trap (14:9)! But 14:13–14 and 30–31 explain that the Lord wants his people to know how total and irreversible their salvation is; it is a completed salvation, from a truly defeated enemy.

3. Disappointment along the way. Why are the Israelites led to a place of disappointment, with no water and then undrinkable water (15:22–23)? What a blow! But then they discover the Lord has been there long before, and has made preparation for their need – 'a tree' (v. 25), planted as long before as it takes a tree to grow. This is an anticipatory providence; the Lord's forward planning. He knows his people will pass this way, so he prepares for their need. We see the same in 17:1 and 6. The water-producing rock is as old as creation itself. Why is it there? Because one day Israel will pass that way and need water – another anticipatory providence.

4. Provision comes with obedience. The Lord is just as competent at providing Israel with food as with water (16: 4, 13). At Marah the Lord uses his provision of water as the occasion to call his people to obedience (15:26), and in the wilderness he uses the provision of manna to test their obedience (16:4). In the case of the manna, as long as they walk in the way of obedience, they walk in the way of provision – gathering what they need each day from an unfailing supply (v. 35); when they forsake obedience, the supply is withdrawn (v. 20).

The Lord's ways frequently seem odd, but they are always purposeful – and merciful. They guard us from dangers he foresees and we do not – from hazards and temptations that would lure us to turn back; bring us experiences and lessons that drive home the wonder and reality of a full and final salvation; and call and entice us to obedience to his word by the sheer wonder of his grace and his thoughtfulness for our welfare.

REFLECTION

As God declared, 'My thoughts are not your thoughts, Nor are your ways My ways' (Is. 55:8).

DAY 17

READ Exodus 14:1–29

The great do-nothing salvation

We noticed the central meaning of Exodus 14 in the note yesterday, but it is important enough to bear repeating. Just notice how the Lord is fully in charge. First, he engineers the situation (vv. 2, 9). When Israel acknowledges their need (v. 10) and the deadly danger (v. 11), and also reveal their unworthiness to have been delivered (v. 12), the Lord then undertakes the whole work of salvation (vv. 13–14). He divides the sea and knows the outcome (vv. 15–18); he moves to protect his unworthy people (vv. 19–20); he has at his command the 'forces' of nature (v. 20); he acts so as to guarantee Egyptian destruction (vv. 21–25); and he brings the waters back (vv. 26), both to destroy and protect (vv. 27–29). Moses sums it all up at the exact mid-point of the narrative (vv. 13–14): Israel's inactivity (they are to remain 'still'), the Lord's salvation and the final end of the deadly enemy. All action is on the Lord's part while Israel does absolutely nothing.

This is always the Bible's message about salvation, so succinctly summed up by Paul in three words: 'He saved us' (Tit. 3:5). Do you remember your school grammar lessons? The subject of a sentence performs the action ('He saved us'); the verb describes the action ('He saved us'); the object of a sentence receives the action ('*He* saved us'). He is totally the Agent; we are totally the recipients; the action is salvation. It is his action: 'by the determined purpose and foreknowledge of God ... crucified' (Acts 2:23). It is our inaction: 'not by works of righteousness which we have done' (Tit. 3:5); 'when we were dead ... not of works' (Eph. 2:5, 9). And it is for salvation: he 'offered one sacrifice for sins forever' (Heb. 10:12). The 'works' to which we are called are not preparatory to faith, nor contributory to faith, but consequent upon faith and giving evidence of faith's reality. Salvation is by grace, through faith – and even that is 'not of yourselves; it is the gift of God' – but we are 'created ... for good works' (Eph. 2:8, 10). Old and New Testaments form one Bible with one message of salvation.

REFLECTION

Rejoice in this: 'O perfect redemption, the purchase of blood; to every believer, the promise of God. The vilest offender who truly believes that moment from Jesus a pardon receives.' [5]

DAY 18

READ Exodus 14:30 – 15:21

A time to sing

This is a carefully constructed passage; take some time to see how it 'hangs together'. 14:30–31 match 15:19. The former deal with divine salvation and Egypt's destruction; the latter with Egypt's destruction and Israel's salvation. They thus form a bracket round Moses' song.

The song begins with victory past (15:1–5) an ends with victories to come (vv. 14–18). In between are two passages focusing on the Lord's hand (see vv. 6, 12). In verses 6–10 we see the Lord's hand in the conquest of human foes; in verses 11–12 of supernatural foes, with the supremacy of the Lord 'among the gods'. The bracketing verses, then, affirm the accomplished reality of our salvation – the song asserts that the victorious Lord who has acted in the past can be trusted for the future. The middle 'hand' section stands for his ability and power to take action and to intervene.

In verse 1 'Then' is the adverb of time: it's that precise moment. Note it! The moment of accomplished salvation was the moment of song. This is the way singing is used throughout the Bible: it is our joyful response to a salvation to which we have contributed nothing. God has so completely undertaken the work of salvation, nothing is left for us but to rejoice in it! (See Judg. 5:1; Ps. 95; 96; 98; Is. 12; 27:1–2; 30:29–32; Rev. 5:9–14.)

When the Bible speaks of other 'gods' (v. 11, cf. 1 Cor. 8:5) it is not affirming their existence but recognising the fact that the nations have objects of worship other than Yahweh – and often, as here, that is a matter of comparison. Yahweh is incomparably different and superior to them (Ps. 96:5; Is. 40:18–20; 44:9–20). This point is important, for we become like the god we worship (Ps. 115:8; Is. 40:31). Moreover God's mighty acts are our persuasive testimony to the world. What he has done convinces them. So in verse 14 the people 'hear' and fear (cf. Josh. 2:9–11). Are we often fearful to offer testimony in case we will be asked questions we can't answer? We must learn to rely on God's truth (telling what he has done) to bring its own conviction.

REFLECTION

Reflect on 15:13–17. The Lord God is our Redeemer, our loving Next-of-kin, who has finished the whole work of salvation. Pray that he will keep you on the path, day by day, to his holy habitation.

Grace and law

Twice in this section we read of Israel grumbling (16:2, 7). This is a mixture of complaint and unbelief. It highlights both their absence of contentment with God's way and their absence of trust that he will provide. Will they never learn? But then will we never learn? The God of the Red Sea is always the God of the Red Sea; the God of the Exodus is always the God of the Exodus; the God who finished the work of salvation is always the saving God. He never changes; never goes back on his word; never leaves his people; and never fails to keep his promises.

It is for this unbelieving, grumbling people that he provides the healing tree (15:25) and the daily manna (16:4). John Newton wrote, 'Daily on the manna feeding which he gives them when they pray'[6] – actually it was when they grumbled! What patience! What forbearance! What love! But the best biblical word is what grace! It was sheer undeserved, unmerited kindness and goodness.

At Marah (15:22–26) the Lord reveals his basic pattern of life to his people: his priority is grace. It always comes first. And grace is always grace – the outreach of unconditional mercy to the unworthy. But the people of grace are the people of law (15:26), that is to say that their gracious God now requires their obedience. Therefore he speaks (v. 26a), revealing first what he considers right (v. 26b) and secondly his law to be kept (v. 26c). Thirdly, he promises blessings consequent on obedience (v. 26d). Grace ... law ... blessing: that is the biblical sequence.

In 16:1–25 this pattern is repeated. Once more the narrative leaves us in no doubt of Israel's unworthiness; grace is therefore grace in its true reality, being love to the loveless and goodness to the undeserving. Grace provides regular food (v. 4), but the provision itself has a built-in test – it must be gathered freshly every day; nothing else will 'work' (v. 20). And, once more, obedience promotes blessing: keeping the Sabbath law is accompanied by undecaying manna (vv. 22–24).

REFLECTION

Were the quails (16:13) just a miracle of provision or also a miracle of providence? Commentators say Israel's journey intersected with the annual migratory path of the quails. Either way the Creator God is on the side of his people.

DAY 20

READ Exodus 16:26 – 17:16

Reliability, providence and availability

'Faith' is not a leap in the dark; it is a leap in the light into the light! It is conviction based on evidence. By the time they reach Exodus 16 the Lord has given his people ample ground for trusting him, and gives us too ample ground for facing life with a basic and immoveable spirit of trust. A spirit of trust, each morning, looks out into the unknown day and says, 'Come what may, I trust you'. A faith meets adversity with, 'Nevertheless, I trust you.'

In today's reading we experience one example in forty years of God's steady reliability in supplying Israel's daily needs (16:16, 35). Every day for forty years the reliable God delivers the day's quota of manna. Never once does Israel have to call heaven to say, 'It hasn't come today.' To trust such a God for our needs is not a leap in the dark, is it? Isn't the evidence for such trust there?

God is reliable. He is also provident – the very word itself means 'forward-looking'. Had he not prepared beforehand a tender-hearted princess to provide a home for Moses (2:5–10)? Had he not grown a tree at Marah in anticipation of Israel's far-future need (15:25)? Had he not built into the fabric of creation itself a water supply in readiness for his pilgrim people (17:6)? Can we not, then, step in confident faith into the unknown future? Wherever our foot touches the ground, we can say, 'The Lord has been here in anticipation of my needs. He has his plans long since laid.'

The message of the final section of our reading (17:8–16) is that, when need arises, the Lord is there to hear and answer prayer. What else can the uplifted hands of Moses signify but a cry heavenwards which brings the Almighty God victoriously into our crises? We too can say, 'The LORD Is My Banner' (v. 15, ESV) – he has come into the thick of the battle to rally his troops, and to give heart and direction to his campaign. The translation of verse 16 is insecure but the most like rendering is: 'For he said, "There is a hand upon the throne of the Lord."' Just imagine it: we lift up our hands and touch his throne!

REFLECTION

Ponder the words of this hymn: prayer 'moves the hand which moves the world, to bring salvation down'.[7]

DAY 21

READ Exodus 18:1–27

The people of the book

We have reached a great dividing line in Exodus. The events of both chapters 18 (see v. 5) and 19 (see vv. 1–2) take place at Sinai. The difference between them is that chapter 19 prepares for what follows, while chapter 18 looks back to what has gone before (see v. 8).

There is another structure to note. In 2:15ff. Moses goes to Jethro; in 18:1ff. Jethro comes to Moses. The passages act like brackets round the whole Exodus event. But there is a huge difference in the two events. Moses fled to Jethro but he did not become a Midianite; he was still 'a stranger in a foreign land' (2:22). Jethro listened to all the Lord had done for his people (18:8) and was converted (vv. 9–10)! Faith comes by hearing (cf. Josh. 10 – 11; Rom. 10:17), and the priest of Midian (18:1) becomes a priest of Israel (v. 12).

Yet the two halves of chapter 18 balance each other. In verses 1–12 Moses speaks and Jethro listens and learns; in verses 13–27 Jethro speaks and Moses learns. It is wholly understandable that people come to Moses to settle their disputes, and to solve their problems and difficulties; it is equally natural for Moses to see this as part of his leadership role. But the result of such a 'one-man band' was that people stood all day waiting for their turn with Moses, and at the day's end he was worn out! Jethro's solution is simple and practical: set up a system whereby each group of ten would have a referee, but with 'higher courts' dealing with fifties, hundreds and thousands of them, and with Moses as the ultimate court of appeal (vv. 19–23). Jethro insists on two things: first, that the scheme must have the Lord's approval (v. 23) – it is not to be judged by common sense or practicality, but only by divine authorisation; and secondly, that the purpose of all the courts is to apply the Lord's statutes and laws, and his ways, truth and life (vv. 20–21) to the Lord's people. The selected 'able men' are to be men of the word of God. The Lord's redeemed people are to be people of the book – like us!

REFLECTION

The word 'statute' is related to the verb 'to engrave', that is, what is cut into the rock for permanency. 'Law' means 'teachings'. 'Way' and 'walk' remind us that the Lord speaks so that we can mould our lives by his truth.

Fixing the foundations

Israel's time at Sinai is recorded in a framework provided by Moses' seven ascents of the mountain to commune with God and bring back word to the people (19:3, 9, 20; 20:21; 24:12; 32:30; 34:2). The three ascents in chapter 19 lay the foundations of what it means to be an Israelite.

First, we see what an Israelite must understand about salvation (vv. 4–6). It is the work of God – who declares 'I did ... I bore' (v. 4; cf. Tit. 3:5; Heb. 10:12). It achieves reconciliation – 'to Myself' (v. 4; cf. Rom. 5:1–2; 2 Cor. 5:18–21). It leads to obedience – the Israelites are to 'obey ... and keep' (v. 5; cf. Acts 5:32; Rom. 6:16, 19). It bestows a privileged relationship – Israel is God's 'treasure' (v. 5; cf. Ex. 19:5; Mal. 3:6–17). It gives access to God – as 'priests' (v. 6; cf. Heb. 10:19–22; 1 Pet. 2:5, 9). And it confers both a status and an objective – holiness (v. 6; cf. 1 Cor. 3:17; 1 Thes. 4:3, 7).

Secondly, we see what an Israelite should understand about revelation (v. 9). The Lord speaks his word, couched in his own words – 'I speak' (cf. 2 Tim. 3:16; Heb. 1:2; 2:3). He acts through chosen channels of his word – 'with you' – setting up a scheme of revelation that can be trusted (cf. 2 Pet. 1:19).

The testimony of verses 10–17 is much more than an interlude: they prepare for the message of the third ascent. To 'meet with God' (v. 17) is a more serious business than we often allow. There should be personal preparation (v. 10), symbolised by washing (cf. John 13:8; 1 Cor. 6:11). The prohibition in verse 15 does not imply that married sex is an impure or defiling thing but rather that coming to God we must take steps to disengage our hearts and focus our love on him.

So we come to the third foundation mark of an Israelite: a sensitivity towards the holiness of God (vv. 20–25). The Lord takes even Moses by surprise in the command to go back and warn the people of this (v. 23) – Moses thought enough had been done to secure the divine holiness against intrusion. But no, the divine holiness is an awesome matter, in no way to be presumed upon (as the priests apparently were doing). Was familiarity breeding carelessness? (See Heb. 10:31; 12:29.) Consider this: it takes all the power of the blood of Christ to allow us to stand before the throne (Rev. 7:14–15).

REFLECTION

Read 1 Peter 1:17–21. To 'fear' (v. 17) is, of course, deep, sensitive reverence – not craven fear. What prompts this reverence (vv. 17a, 18–19)?

Responding to grace

The Ten Commandments are not a ladder of merit by which we seek to climb into God's 'good books', winning our way into his favour by our works. Exodus 20:2 firmly puts God's action in salvation first. He speaks his commands to us not in order that we may be saved but because he has already saved us, and now the same grace which saved us teaches us how to respond in grateful obedience. This relationship between grace and law, between salvation and responsive obedience, remains the same right through the Bible. The Ten Commandments themselves present a rounded and balanced pattern for life, as the following simple outline shows:

A. Spiritual (commandments 1–4)
   a. Thoughts (commandments 1–2)
   b. Words (commandment 3)
   c. Deeds (commandment 4)
B. Domestic (commandment 5)
C. Social (commandments 6–10)
   a. Deeds (commandments 6–8)
   b. Words (commandment 9)
   c. Thoughts (commandment 10)

It is mistaken to think that the Decalogue deals only with externalities, awaiting Jesus to make them apply also to the heart (Mt. 5:12, 28). See how it opens and closes with our thoughts, spiritual and social. Has the Lord our sole and total loyalty and commitment?

The above outline takes note of the different way the fifth commandment is expressed compared to the first four commands – with a positive instruction rather than a prohibition ('Honour ...', v. 12) and that it is emphasised by having a promise of 'long' life attached to it (cf. Eph. 6:1–4). After our 'duty to God', our domestic life and relationships are our first concern and responsibility (cf. Mark 7:9–13; 1 Tim. 3:4–5).

The essential point of the commandments – indeed the whole law of God – is spelled out in Leviticus 19. That chapter is a veritable jumble of topics – rather like life itself! But each regulation is enforced by the reminder 'I am the LORD'. Given that 'LORD' stands for the divine name (Ex. 3:13–15), 'I am the LORD' is equivalent to 'I AM WHO I AM'. Each commandment – and the whole Decalogue – comes to us not arbitrarily but because Yahweh is what he is. It reflects and expresses him. Keeping his commandments makes us like him.

REFLECTION

Contemplate further the glorious and enriching truths of God's Law by reading Psalm 19:7–11.

DAY 24

READ Exodus 20:22 – 21:36

Grace and law – again!

This passage addresses various topics. First, the place of blessing (20:22–26). Before a single law is pronounced, he wants them to know the way of blessing (20:24). This involves burnt offerings (which express holding nothing back, Gen. 22:8–12, and make atonement, Lev. 1:4), and making 'peace offerings' (or 'fellowship offerings', NIV). These are the essential elements of the burnt and sin offerings, but the 'fellowship' or 'peace' offering also includes, characteristically, a fellowship meal (cf. Deut. 12:7) where the fellowship offering is referred to as a freewill offering.

Secondly, there are laws about indentured service (Ex. 21:1–11). We must understand though, that Hebrew has no word for 'slave' (in the post-Christian, Caribbean sense) but only a word for 'servant'. It is simply ignorance to accuse the Old Testament of countenancing 'slavery'. Indeed verse 5 indicates that 'service' was far from oppressive – there had to be legislation to cater for servants who wanted to stay as such!

Thirdly, we have a section dealing with violence against the person (vv. 12–27). The Hebrew 'due process of law' catered for what we call 'degrees of murder', but had no qualms about the death penalty. The wording 'eye for eye' (v. 24, known as *Lex Talionis*) needs careful thought. It is often referred to as if it represented the utmost savagery. But what does it actually say? It states that the punishment must exactly match the crime – no more and no less! It vividly expresses a foundational principle of all just jurisprudence. The English law of hanging for stealing a sheep happened not because the Lex *Talionis* was in force but because it had been forgotten!

Fourthly, there are decrees concerning the control of animals (vv. 28–36). The law of God penetrated into every aspect of life – it would be interesting to apply some of these laws to dangerous driving! No area of life lies outside our obedience to him.

REFLECTION

21:30 helps us understand the great concept of redemption: the 'sum of money' demanded is* kopher, *from the verb* kaphar, *meaning 'to cover'. In other words it is 'the covering price' – the payment that 'covers' the debt. Parallel to this, 'to redeem his life' represents the Hebrew for 'the ransom price for his life'. Price-paying lies at the root of the biblical idea of redeeming.

DAY 25

READ Exodus 22:1–31

Owners, guardians and monotheists

22:1–17 comes under the heading of property and ownership but in various senses verses 1–6 rest in the assumption that we have a right to private property, and that this right must be safeguarded by sanctions against theft (vv. 1–4) or wilful damage (vv. 5–6). In Old Testament law there is no sense in which one size fits all. Different cases require different responses, but theft itself is always wrong, and restitution must be paid – not to the Treasury but to the injured party.

Guardianship, where goods or money are entrusted to someone's care (vv. 7–13), rests on an assumption of integrity on the part of the person trusted. Verse 11 opens a window into a society of trust in which it can be taken for granted that a person's word is his bond.

The case of the unmarried daughter (vv. 16–17) – though possibly according more authority to the father than is the norm today – is an issue of guardianship since the parent is the responsible guardian as long as she is under his roof. Pre-marital sex created an obligation to marry – and indissoluble marriage at that (Deut. 22:28–29)!

Offences against monotheism attracted the death penalty, being as they were primary violations of the Decalogue. This obviously applies in verses 18 and 20, but also in verse19 because 'bestiality' was a feature of Canaanite fertility cults. But the particular nature of Israelite monotheism exerted its own distinctive requirements. First is the need to live in a way that reflects the nature of our redemption (v. 21). The situation from which we were redeemed must make us especially concerned for those who are still as we once were. Secondly is the obligation to relate to people in a way that matches the Lord's attitude towards them (vv. 23, 27). The helpless and resourceless (v. 22) are Yahweh's special concern. The debtor must be protected from the 'loan shark' (vv. 22–27). Thirdly is the requisite to be holy – to display in every way the difference and distinctiveness proper to those who are *the* LORD's (v. 31).

REFLECTION

To be holy (v. 31) means 'to be separated' to one's God – to belong to his sphere of reality, live by his rules, and reflect what he is and what he wishes.

Present ... permanent ... prospective

Exodus 23 concludes the Book of the Covenant. The laws (21:1 – 23:9) are bookended by the preface about the altar (20:22–26) – how and where the Lord comes to us (v. 24) – and the epilogue about the rhythm of our days (23:10–29) – with instructions for the seventh year, the seventh day and the three annual feasts where the Israelites come to him.

This chapter also looks into the future: an angel (vv. 20–26) and 'My fear' (vv. 27–33) go ahead of Israel, bringing them into the Promised Land. In both of these sections the common theme is that Israel is the exclusive people of God (vv. 24, 32).

Our reading of the chapter is easier if we observe the way it all belongs together. The introductory section, when Moses is at Sinai in preparation for the covenant (19:1–25), is matched by the concluding section, when Moses is again at Sinai, this time to ratify the covenant (24:1–8). Within this balanced presentation, the Decalogue (20:1–17) matches the Book of the Laws (21:1 – 23:9).

If we look at Exodus 23 in detail, we are to be people of integrity (vv. 1–2) and charity (vv. 3, 6, 9). In verse 3 'poor' means without resources; in verse 6 a different Hebrew word is used, meaning 'vulnerable', that is liable to be pushed around by stronger forces and 'interests'; in verse 9 the 'stranger' is the resident alien, the refugee, the person needing care and attention.

Life is to be subordinate to a divinely imposed rhythm (vv. 10–19). The 'land-sabbath' is to take place every seven years (vv. 10–11; cf. Lev. 25:1–7). What a colossal act of faith: a year of dependence on what the Lord causes to grow! It is the very denial of capitalistic greed! Notice too the stress on the humanitarian aspect of the Sabbath (v. 12) – and its bearing on Sunday trading! More particularly observe that Exodus sees this rhythm only in relation to our devotion to one God (v. 13) – a theme carried on in verses 24 and 32.

The special being called 'The Angel of the LORD' is both the Lord and distinct from the Lord (as passages like Genesis 16:7–14 show). In Exodus 23:21 he possesses the Lord's Name and dignity; in 33:1–2 he accommodates the Lord's holy presence to live among a sinful people. He is a preview of the Lord Jesus Christ.

REFLECTION

In Psalm 34:7 the angel takes up residence in a 'mobile home' so as to be always alongside us.

Immovably secure

The picture in verse 4 is not perhaps detailed in the way we would wish. Yet the whole of Israel – the redeemed people, God's firstborn son – is represented by twelve pillars, and we are at liberty to think of the altar (the divine presence) that Moses also builds as being encircled by those who have been brought to God (19:4). The stonework used for the pillars stands for permanency; twelve stands for totality. A telling portrayal of what has been achieved – acceptation into the actual presence of God – is fixed there in perpetuity.

Israel was brought out of Egypt by the blood of the lamb; the blood of sacrifice holds them secure in the presence of their Redeemer God (vv. 5–6). The burnt offerings stand for commitment and atonement; the peace offerings for acceptance and fellowship. The way Moses uses the blood, in verses 6–8, completes the imagery. Remember how at the Passover the Lord came in wrath but passed over in peace the blood-marked houses (12:13). Wrath was satisfied and peace established by the evidence that a substitute had died. Blood as such symbolised life laid down and terminated in death, and first exercised its wondrous effect Godward. In the same way in Exodus 24 the blood is first applied Godward (v. 6), and this is the reason why Israel is immovably secure: the blood satisfies wrath and secures peace.

But the primary characteristic of the redeemed is obedience to the word of God. For this reason Moses reads the Book of the Covenant and the people respond with a commitment to obey (v. 7). Yet no sooner have they committed themselves to obey than the remaining blood is sprinkled on them (vv. 7–8). In other words, while they commit themselves to obedience, the precious blood of their substitute covers all their shortcomings, deficiencies and failures. We walk in the light of God's word and the blood of Jesus, God's Son, keeps on cleansing us from all sin (1 John 1:7). The life of the redeemed is always dependent on sacrificial blood; we are the recipients and trustees of the revealed word of God; and our life of obedience is still covered by the blood that saved us.

REFLECTION

Rejoice in the words of this hymn: 'There is a fountain filled with blood drawn from Emmanuel's veins. And sinners plunged beneath that flood lose all their guilty stains ... Dear dying Lamb, Thy precious blood shall never lose its power till all the ransomed church of God be saved, to sin no more.'[8]

DAY 28

READ Exodus 25:1–40

The meeting place

The Lord commands a dwelling place for himself (v. 8) and then immediately commands the ark (v. 10). In a word, that is what the tabernacle is for – to house the ark; the ark secures the purpose for which the tabernacle is intended (v. 22): the place to meet the indwelling God.

The ark is to be overlaid and inlaid with gold (v. 11), which, among the metals of the tabernacle, stands for all that is special and glorious: the very presence of God. Inside the ark is to be placed the 'tablets of the covenant law' (v. 16, NIV), called 'the Testimony' in the NKJV because they testify to who and what the Lord is, to what he requires of his redeemed people, and, by implication, to our need before him as those who have broken his law.

Next, however, is 'the mercy seat' (v. 17): a wholly golden 'lid', made to the exact measurements of the Ark so as to cover it precisely. In Hebrew it is the *kapporeth* or 'covering', but the parent verb *kaphar*, while in its simple form means 'to cover', in its developed form means 'to pay the covering price' – as we saw on Day 24. The *kapporeth*, then, is 'the atonement-covering' or 'the price-covering-the-debt'. This name comes into its own on the Day of Atonement, when the atoning blood is sprinkled on the mercy seat (Lev. 16:15–16), and the atonement cover receives the price that covers the sins and transgressions of Israel. The symbolism is of the broken law covered by the sprinkled price of a substitutionary life laid down in death.

Integral to the mercy seat are the cherubim figures turned inward and gazing downwards (Ex. 25:18–20). Ezekiel 1:10 reveals the cherubim as having four faces, representing the whole of creation – that of a lion, the greatest of wild beasts; an eagle, the greatest of birds; an ox, the greatest of domestic beasts; and a man, the crown of creation. The cherubim are both earthly and unearthly, because the whole of heaven and earth is focused on the wonder of the atonement.

REFLECTION

Consider these words: 'Be thou my shield and hiding place that, sheltered by thy side, I may my fierce accuser face, and tell him thou hast died!'[9]

DAY 29

READ Exodus 26 – 27

(especially 26:1, 31–33, 36; 27:16) and 28:4–6, 8, 15

A colourful scene

I am sure that every item of the tabernacle has a message to tell (cf. Heb. 9:5). Sometimes the symbols are explained; sometimes we apply our best thought and imagination to fathom their meaning. The essential thing is to understand symbols only illustrate and clarify truths plainly stated elsewhere in the Bible.

So what about the colours used in the tabernacle? They run right through our verses today, don't they? Yes, but not haphazardly. The curtains covering the whole tabernacle are blue, purple and scarlet, plus the white of fine linen (26:1), which are the colours used to express the identity of the whole dwelling. The same colours mark the way in – the door of the court (27:16), the entrance of the tent (26:36), and the curtain into the Holy of Holies (vv. 31–33) – and finally the distinctively priestly garment (28:4–5), the ephod (v. 6) and its associated woven band (v. 8) and breastplate (v. 15).

Each of these items is a whole study in itself, but, standing back from the whole, we can follow the clue given in Hebrews 10:20: 'the veil, that is, His flesh'. As one chorus puts it well, the Lord Jesus Christ is the 'way back to God from the dark paths of sin' and 'a door that is open and you may go in'.[10] Through him we come into his courts. Just as priests enter the tabernacle, we, through the rent veil of Jesus' flesh and by his priestly work, are welcome into the Holiest place itself. At the instant, split-second of his death, the veil was torn from top to bottom (Mark 15:37–38). All this the tabernacle expresses in the symbolism of its colours: the door of the court, the entrance of the tent and the tent itself are overshadowed in blue, purple, scarlet and white linen, together with the lovely veil of the Holy of Holies, now torn in two through Jesus' sacrificial death, who is the Great High Priest himself who 'obtained eternal redemption' for us (Heb. 9:12). He alone, in the unity of one perfect Person, is the blue of heavenly origin, the purple of royal lineage and dignity, the scarlet of the atoning sacrifice for sin, and the white linen of unstained purity and moral majesty.

REFLECTION

Stand in the tabernacle and look up: Jesus is over us, but also those coloured curtains are all around us: we are 'in Christ', where we find redemption (Rom. 3:24); no condemnation (Rom. 8:1); inseparable love (Rom. 8:35); status as a child of God (Gal. 3:26); every spiritual blessing (Eph. 1:4); and our life is hid with Christ in God (Col. 3:3).

Our great high priest

Clothing expresses the character and purpose of the wearer. In Joshua 5:13 – 6:2, the 'Commander of the army of the LORD' (v. 14) comes, with the Lord dressed for the part (v. 13). The dress declares the person. So Aaron wears the priestly garments the Lord designs for holiness, glory and beauty, to declare (in this case) what the wearer should be.

First, a priest is qualified to wear the ephod (v. 6; cf. 1 Sam. 2:28; 22:18). The ephod does not seem to have any other significance than to be the distinctive priestly dress. (We do not know whether it was short, like a waistcoat, or longer like a kaftan.) Secondly, the back and front of the ephod are joined by shoulder straps on which are the engraved stones (vv. 7, 9–13), so that on his shoulders the priest carries the names of his people: a picture of the final reality of our Priest living for ever to make intercession for us (Heb. 7:25). The third garment, the woven band (v. 8), keeps the ephod in place, and the fourth, the breastpiece (vv. 15–30), is loosely held to the front of the ephod by gold cords linking it to the shoulder stones and gold rings linking it to the woven band. The addition of gold in the priest's case marks him as divine – a requirement which, like all the others, was unfulfilled until Jesus came.

The priest's carrying of names on his heart before the Lord (v. 29) is another way of saying that he is responsible for their welfare. The stones put in the breastpiece and called Urim and Thummin (v. 30; literally, 'the lights and the perfections') stand for the ideal reality of the Lord's people as he sees them. Functionally, these stones were a mechanism of guidance whereby the Lord answered 'yes' or 'no' questions (1 Sam. 23:2) or refused to answer (1 Sam. 14:37). These particular verses do not mention the stones but the reference to the ephod (1 Sam. 23:5, 6, 9) implies their use. In verses 29–30 the phrase 'breastplate of judgment' has the basic meaning of decision-making. The priest is the divinely intended decision-maker of his people, responsible for bringing them safely to their homeland.

The fifth priestly garment is the robe of the ephod (vv. 31–35), designed for the practical purpose of assuring hearers that the priest is alive and active. The sixth garment, the turban or headpiece, is only mentioned as the place where the seventh item, the beautiful medallion of holiness, is set (vv. 36–38), anticipating the holy perfection of Jesus (Heb. 5:8–10; 7:27–28). But as the Holy One our Priest can indeed bear our iniquity (Ex. 28: 38), because he meets the requirement for the lamb to be perfect (12:5).

REFLECTION

The Lord Jesus Christ is our 'wisdom' (1 Cor. 1:24, 30; Col. 2:2–3).

DAY 31

READ Exodus 29:1–37

The making of a priest

It is not wearing priestly robes (vv. 4–9) that makes Aaron and his sons priests: the robes are a declaration of intent and a statement of the ideal. What actually inducts them into the priestly office is the regular complement of sacrifices – the sin-offering (vv. 10–14) for atonement and forgiveness (cf. Lev. 5:13); the burnt offering (vv. 15–18) of acceptance and atonement (cf. Lev. 1:4), holding nothing back from God (Gen. 22:8, 12); and the 'consecration' or peace offering (vv. 19–22, 26–27).

In each case the worshipper is required to lay his hand on the head of the sacrificial animal (vv. 10, 15, 19). This is an act of identification. On the Day of Atonement all the sins of Israel pass to the goat by the laying on of hands (Lev. 16:21–22). A deep substitution is effected. The old, sinful Israel goes to the wilderness, never to be seen; the new forgiven Israel remains. Laying on his hand, the offerer in effect is saying, 'This is I – dying as the wages of sin, holding nothing back from God, concentrating myself wholly to him.' It is our position when we can sing, 'My faith would lay her hand on that dear head of thine while, like a penitent, I stand and there confess my sin.'[11] All our demerit is reckoned to Jesus; all his perfection to us.

'A ram of consecration' (v. 22) is expressed in the Hebrew idiom 'for it is a ram of filling'. The full expression for consecration is 'to fill one's hands'. Just like we say of someone whose life seems very demanding, 'He/she has his/her hands full', so consecration is a life filled for God in every department – hence the blood being put on the ears, thumbs and toes of Aaron and his sons (v. 20). It is a life wholly active for him in what we hear, do and where we go – and in what we refuse to hear and do, and where we refuse to go.

After all that, Aaron and his sons are required to spend seven days in retreat (vv. 35–37). They might have been keen to get started on their new life; the Lord is in no hurry. Every ministry they could now offer is essential for the people; yet never mind, there is no hurry. They are to take time to become the people God wants them to be.

REFLECTION

Isaiah 50:4 is a forecast of the Lord Jesus, the perfect disciple and Servant of the Lord. Ponder his morning timetable.

Meeting God

Without doubt 'regularly' in 29:42 (NIV) should be 'perpetually' or 'continually', the standard meaning of the word. The burnt offering is always there, always in operation. Leviticus 6:9 speaks of it on the altar 'all night until morning', and then that 'the fire ... shall be kept burning ... it shall not be put out' (vv. 11–12). Verse 13 literally adds: 'a perpetual fire shall burn ... never go out'. It speaks of perpetual atonement, and of a people perpetually represented as holding nothing back in their devotion to the Lord. This is the situation in which the Lord is pleased to meet with and speak to his people (Ex. 29:42), and in which he finds the fulfilment of what he purposed in their redemption (v. 46).

Before we go on (as Exodus does) to the beautiful golden altar of incense (30:1–10), we must pause to recall those times when we say we 'are getting nothing out of' our Bible reading, and it seems as if God has stopped talking to us. We need to ask ourselves the question: 'How is it with us and the great Burnt Offering? Are we living in close unitedness with the Atonement?' Can we sing, 'Jesus, keep me near the cross, there a precious fountain; free to all, a healing stream, flows from Calvary's mountain. In the cross, in the cross be my glory ever till my ransomed soul shall find rest beyond the river'?[12] Are we living in the spirit of holding nothing back?

Moving on to the golden altar, we must see this in the wonderful balance of Scripture – Exodus 29 ends with the Lord coming to us to speak to us, and chapter 30 opens with the provision for us to come to God for him to meet with us (v. 6; cf. 30:36). Incense as a symbol is not, as such, explained in the Bible, but surely the picture is clear enough: outside the veil the altar stands, but functionally its sweet savour penetrates the veil – 'a perpetual incense before the LORD' (v. 8) and something the Lord considers 'most holy' (v. 10); it is exceedingly precious to him and reminds him of us and our needs. Hebrews 9:3–5 is too versed in Scripture to think the golden altar was within the veil, yet it places it there! In other words, though outside the veil, its sweet and holy influence brings us into the very presence of the Most Holy God.

REFLECTION

Scripture calls us to be an 'aroma' of Christ in the world (2 Cor. 2:15–16) – a task to which we are equal through the way we handle the word of God (v. 17). Our care for each other in the gospel is 'a fragrant offering ... pleasing to God' (Phil. 4:18, NIV 1984).

DAY 33

READ Exodus 30:22 – 31:18

A suitable place, equipped people and regulated life

It may help to look back quickly and see the tabernacle chapters as a whole – not just one thing after another! In 24:12 Moses ascends Sinai; in 31:18 he descends. 25:1–9, detailing the tabernacle materials, matches 31:1–11, the tabernacle makers; 25:10 – 27:21, listing the furnishings, is balanced by 30:1–38, outlining the fitness (by anointing) of the furnishings. The central 28:1 – 29:46 focuses on the priesthood.

The anointing oil (30:22–33) is a symbol of the Holy Spirit. Everything about the tabernacle is as God wishes it (25:9; 31:11), but it is not fit for his service until it is set apart in holiness.

In 30:34 the focus turns to incense. According to Psalm 141:2 prayer is 'as incense', but incense as such is not a symbol of prayer; in Revelation 8:3 incense is offered 'with the prayers'. The verb form of incense (*qatar*, meaning 'to make to smoke') is used of the sacrifices (see Ex. 30:20), and the burnt offering has, literally, a 'sweet smell' to God (see Gen. 8:21). Thus the smoke and scent of the incense perpetuate the influence of the sacrifices. The incense itself is kindled by fire from the bronze altar (Ex. 27:1–7), which was the place of sacrifice, so that, in a sense, its smoke is the smoke of the sacrifices. Wrapped in that smoke the High Priest brings his sin offering into the Holy of Holies, shielding him from the dangerous glory of the Lord (v. 13). '... we', says Paul, 'are to God the fragrance of Christ' (2 Cor. 2:15) – the Christ of Calvary is the cloud of incense in which we appear in the presence of God.

In the next section we see that not only Bezalel and Aholiab but all the artisans are gifted by God for the work (Ex. 31:6). In the versatility of the operations of the Holy Spirit (v. 3) there is no aspect of our lives in which we cannot look for his anointing that God may be glorified.

At the end of the chapter we may wonder why the Sabbath regulations are repeated here (cf. 35:1–3). Maybe, with the huge volume of work the tabernacle team faced, they might have felt excused from the Sabbath, or that such holy work was itself exempt? That is not so! The Sabbath is a 'sign' (vv. 13, 17); it is 'holy' and 'a perpetual covenant' (vv. 14, 16); and it is enforced by the severest penalty (v. 15).

REFLECTION

We do not have the Sabbath regulation (Col. 2:16) but we do have the creation ordinance of the one day in seven.

DAY 34

READ Exodus 32:1–35

The great sin

Up to Exodus 32 we might say Paul's words in Romans 4:15 applied: 'where there is no law there is no transgression'. Clearly when Israel pledged total obedience (Ex. 19:8), their hearts were in the right place (cf. Deut. 5:28–29), but they had not faced up either to the law or to themselves! The incident of the golden calf brings home to them their situation as sinners (33:1–6)

The way the story is told fashions its own lessons:

1. Impatience is a dangerous game (32:1)! A quiet spirit that waits confidently needs cultivation (cf. Ps. 130:5–8; Is. 40:31).

2. Do not neglect the strength of fellowship (vv. 2–6). Ought not Aaron to have been aware of his own inadequacies as a leader? Moses seems to have been, since he appointed a team leadership in his absence (24:14). Why did Aaron not bring Hur into the equation?

3. Our only recourse when faced with the wrath of God is to run to God (vv. 7–14). Divine wrath is easy to understand: turning to a false god is equivalent to identifying the true God with our falsity (v. 8). Imagine how, after all that they had seen, learned and experienced of Yahweh, they could look at the absurdity of a gold 'thing' and effectively say, 'This is Yahweh'!! Is it any wonder he was outraged? But Yahweh will always be faithful to his work of redemption (v. 11) – Israel is still his redeemed; it was for them he descended to Egypt. He will always work for the honour of his own Name (v. 12), and keep the covenant promises he has made (v. 13).

4. To break one commandment is to break the whole law (vv. 15–19; cf. Jas. 2:9–11).

5. Turning to another god is ludicrously inexcusable (vv. 20–24) and inevitably leads to loose conduct (v. 25).

6. The time when others are defecting is the time to stand up and be counted (vv. 26–32; cf. Rom. 9:1–3).

7. Nothing diverts the Lord from his purpose of saving his people (vv. 34–35). Notice the use of 'Now' in verse 34: now, in this day of sin and deserved wrath, the Promised Land is still Israel's destination.

REFLECTION

Rejoice in our security in Christ (John 10:28–29; 14:1–3; Eph. 2:4–6; Rev. 7:14–15).

The other tent

Whatever do they want another tent for (33:7)? Isn't the tabernacle in all its glory enough for them? Well, no! They do need another tent – and so do you and I!

Moses has just spent forty days and nights alone with God (Deut. 9:9). He is so delighted in that divine Presence with him that he says he would prefer to stay in the wilderness rather than go forward to the Promised Land without it (Ex. 33:15)! Very likely he has already experienced in himself something of the personal transformation that is plainly evident after his second forty-day sojourn with the Lord (34:28, 30). At any rate it is for this reason that Moses, literally, 'used to take a tent and pitch it outside the camp ... calling it the "tent of meeting"' (33:7 NIV 1984). And it is a place to which anyone seeking the Lord 'used to go'. Public, corporate worship is one thing. By the Lord's will it is catered for by the tabernacle and its sacrifices. Personal, private time with God is another thing, and it is for this that Moses pitches the second tent. Notice the connection: following the second stay on the mountain (34:28), Moses' face is shining because 'he talked with Him [the Lord]' (v. 29). Moses also speaks with the Lord when he goes to the tent (33:9): it is a place of personal communion with God.

The tabernacle services are at set times, but Moses exercises personal responsibility in going to the tent. 33:8 and 34:34 say 'whenever', implying it is whenever Moses decides to or choses to. But whenever he does so, the Lord graciously affirms the situation by coming to meet him and securing the privacy of the meeting (33:9). 34:34 says Moses goes in to speak with the Lord, but when he comes out he brings with him what the Lord had said to him. It is a real meeting: Moses desires it, and the Lord makes it effective.

Now do you see why they needed a second tent, and why I say that you and I need one too? We each need a place of private meeting with God – just him and me. For us, of course, no tent is needed – just a simple turning to God. The angel, the Lord Jesus, welcomes us into his tent and makes room for us (Ps. 34:7).

REFLECTION

May we echo these words: 'Like Jesus, like Jesus; I want to be like Jesus.'[13] Follow his example in Isaiah 50:4 and Mark 1:35. (Well, perhaps do not rise 'before daylight', but say fifteen minutes before you usually get up!)

DAY 36

READ Exodus 35:1 – 36:7

Priorities

In Exodus chapters 36–40 we find three additional tabernacle Lists – making four in total. We have already read the List of Specification (chapters 25–31), setting out what is to be provided. Next come the List of Manufacture (chapters 36–39), detailing how each item is to be made; the List of Construction (40:1–16), describing how to put it all together; and the List of Erection (40:17–33), where it is finally built. How very important the tabernacle is, then, to command such space and repeated detail!

This is underlined by another statistic – 35:1 states the principle governing the whole enterprise: 'which the LORD has commanded you to do'. This insistence on divine authorisation and detailed design comes twenty-three times – including, in chapter 39, seven times of individual articles, and, in chapter 40, seven times in the course of erection. We should understand this as a mandate to study every detail of the tabernacle: everything is where and what it is by divine direction. The Lord planned, directed and oversaw it all. There is truth in every symbol, and there is a central truth in the whole – the tabernacle achieves the purpose the Lord had in mind when he set about redeeming his people from Egypt: 'that I may dwell among them' (29:46).

Israel is a tent-dwelling people; the Lord will live in his tent alongside them. We see this worked out in Numbers 2 in how Israel is to set up camp. Think of the camp like a great cross, with the Judah tribes stretching out in a line east, the Reuben tribes to the south, the Ephraim tribes on the west, and the Dan tribes northwards. But at the exact centre of the crossing is the Lord's tent, the tabernacle. The Lord is in the middle of his people. Everything else is an adjunct to that great reality – the sacrifices, the mercy seat, the work of the Priests and Levites; all else is in the interest of enabling and securing the presence of the Holy One among sinners.

This is the problem Haggai faces when his people turn from building the Lord's house: do they not want the Lord at the centre of their lives (Hag. 1:2–4)? Moses' people do – look at their response on the great gift day (36:4–7)! And should we not go all out to avoid and banish whatever offends his presence and to cultivate everything that he desires and that delights him?

REFLECTION

We are given another priority in 35:1–3, which is the last of seven times the Sabbath law is referred to. The Lord is serious about the 'apartness' of his holy day.

DAY 37

READ Exodus 37:1–29

The undeflected God

We should read through Exodus 37 just to revel in the sheer beauty of the Lord's tent – gold is everywhere in sight, with beautifully crafted artefacts, and the table and incense altar are bathed in the shimmering light of the seven-branched lampstand. Of course, in the days when the tabernacle stood, only the High Priest entered to trim the lamps and burn the incense (Lev. 16:1–19). Then when, once a year, he went beyond the second veil, to offer his own sin offering, all was shrouded in the incense cloud. Yet when, in his character as representing the ideal Priest, he offered the people's sin offering, there was no incense cloud and doubtless he saw the golden mercy seat and the cherubim (Lev. 16:13, 15). But Scripture allows us to fill our eyes with the beauty of it all and to marvel at it; this is part of our privilege, so let us read and enjoy it.

Our memories, however, will be telling us that chapter 37 is identical with chapter 25, so we may begin to wonder why it is necessary to repeat all the same details in this second list. But just pause for a moment. What has happened between the two lists? The great sin of the golden calf! Israel's continuance before God has been brought into jeopardy (32:10); they have become aware of themselves as a sinful nation; and Moses has entertained doubt if the Lord could continue to be with them (34:9). This is precisely the point – and a most important one. So much has changed, so much has been made uncertain, but the Lord continues, undeterred, on his way. What he plans remains the same; word for word he proceeds to do exactly what he said he was going to do. It is not that the Israelites' sin does not matter, or that it is not serious, or that he is simply prepared to look the other way. It is much more marvellous. He is God, and his forward planning takes account of their sin and need before him. Indeed, far from needing to revise his plans for the tabernacle, those very plans come into their own as God's intended way of handling Israel's sin and admitting them, though sinners, safe into his presence. So the tabernacle details are repeated, word or word, article for article, and duty for duty. We change; he does not change!

REFLECTION

Ponder the unchanging nature of God (Num. 23:19; Mal. 3:6; 1 Cor. 1:8–9; Heb. 1:10–12; Jas. 1:17).

DAY 38

READ Exodus 38:1–31

The chosen metals

Every detail of the tabernacle is divinely commanded, including the fabrics and materials to be used. Nothing is left to human choice, nor does anything need adjustment in the course of construction. The chosen metals are gold, silver and bronze (vv. 24, 25, 29), and each is used appropriately to its place in the whole scheme.

The altar of burnt offering is of bronze (v. 30). It is the place where the fire of divine holy wrath burns – but is propitiated and satisfied by the substitutionary offerings made there. Bronze therefore symbolises the satisfied and propitiated wrath of God. All the court curtains rest on bronze, including the pillars of the gate screen and the entrance curtain of the tent (27:16–17; 26:36–37). Everything thus rests on a basis of substitution and propitiation, especially the entrance into the court and into the tent.

The silver used (vv. 25–28) is the redemption money of Israel (cf. 30:13–16; Lev. 27:6; Num. 3:43–51), giving silver the symbolic significance of redemption, the payment of the covering price. All the hooks from which the curtains hang are silver (27:10); the wall boards of the tabernacle rest on silver sockets (26:18–19) and so do the pillars of the veil of the Holy of Holies (26:32).

Redemption is that on which we depend and is the basis on which we rest, giving us our secure position before God. Therefore the closer in we penetrate to where the Lord himself dwells in holiness, the more everything is of gold – the first metal of the three (38:24). The boards are overlaid with gold (26:29), as are the pillars of the door curtain and of the screen curtain of the Holy of Holies (26:32, 37).

The only non-gold elements in the tabernacle are the bronze bases of the door screen, and the silver bases of the boards and of the inner sanctuary screen. In other words, we come via the way of substitutionary sacrifice and redemption payment into the pure gold of the divine presence. The source of much if not all this valuable metal is what Israel brought out as legitimate plunder from Egypt (12:35–36): the redeemed consecrate all the fruits of redemption to obey what the Lord commands, and to welcome in his presence at the centre of their lives.

REFLECTION

Jesus is our Temple (John 2:19–21), our Entrance (Heb. 10:19–22), and our Forerunner (Heb. 6:19–20).

DAY 39

READ Exodus 39:42–43; 40:16–33

Moses the finisher

Look at the beginning and end of this portion: it begins with total obedience and ends with total accomplishment - and in between says seven times that all was as the Lord commanded. This is something by no means true of all the Bible characters. The delightful Joshua ended his days with much land yet to be possessed (Josh. 13:1). Samson began to save Israel (Judg. 13:5) but, great buffoon that he was, frittered his life and opportunities away. David did well until, at the halfway mark, he met Bathsheba and everything began to fall apart, so that in his frightful death-bed commission to Solomon there were loose ends still to be tied (1 Kgs. 2:5–9). In contrast, Nehemiah was a finisher (Neh. 6:15). Paul had a driving ambition to be a finisher (Acts 20:24) - and he succeeded (2 Tim. 4:7). Pre-eminently, to the praise of God and our eternal security, the Lord Jesus Christ is the supreme example of the Finisher (John 17:4; 19:28, 30; Heb. 5:9; 9:12; 10:12).

With what patience Moses carries through the tabernacle work. He receives the commission (25:8). In the original language there then is an abundance of the second personal singular ('you') verbs throughout chapters 25–30 that represent Moses as the great doer. Bezalel is called by God (31:2) but he and his team are directed by Moses (36:2). It is Moses who inspects and approves their work (39:43), who is put in charge of the construction (40:2) and who personally directs the details of the process of erection (40:18). All this is done with itemised care and planning. The recalcitrance of his people means that Moses is fighting his way forwards at every point. He has every incentive to give up in the face of daunting odds, but he does not.

If we were to try to stand beside Moses the day the tabernacle is completed, words spring to mind: dedication, obedience (of the gritted teeth variety), persistence, attention to detail and devotion. We would have to write them all somehow into Moses' obituary. We should covet them for ourselves. Pilgrimage is not picnicking.

REFLECTION

Remember the admonishment: 'Let not the one who puts on his armour boast like the one who takes it off' (1 Kgs. 20:11). Stand firm in your armour of God (Eph. 6:13).

Yes ... no ... yes ...

Does Moses get a surprise when he finds the way into the tabernacle barred against him (v. 35)? He has been in and out of the great tent in the course of superintending its erection, and has been scrupulous in observing its requirements (vv. 31–32), but now that the divine Resident has taken up occupation there (v. 34), everything is different. The people of the golden calf cannot find a place with the holy Glory. The Lord is certainly 'at home' among his people, but his house is not open to callers.

Thankfully, however, so much remains unchanged (vv. 36–38). As the hymn puts it, 'Round each habitation hovering, see the cloud and fire appear! For a glory and a covering showing that the Lord is near'.[14] The faithful God, just as before, marks his presence, protects his people, oversees their pilgrimage and guides them home, ever present, ever watchful and ever caring.

But the presence is a holy presence. The cloud which proclaims also hides; the fire which lights is the fire of holy wrath against sin. The tabernacle is complete, but it cannot be open. This is the point at which it is important to read from Exodus into Leviticus. (The first five books of the Bible are continuous: see how Numbers 1:1 follows Leviticus 27:34, and how Deuteronomy 1:1 picks up from Numbers 36:13). In Leviticus 1:2 the verb 'brings' actually means 'to bring near', and the word 'offering' comes from the same verb. In order to make this wording clearer, we could render the verse as: 'When anyone brings near a bringing-near to the Lord, you shall bring near your bringing-near ...' Do you see the significance of this? In effect, the Lord is saying to Moses, 'You can't come near but I provide for you a bringing-near.' The Holy One in all his glory is unapproachable (Ex. 40:34–35), but, with the sacrifice he has appointed (for 'atonement', Lev. 1:4) his people can approach, and be accepted.

This is certainly what the tabernacle is all about – it is a provision by which sinners can safely enjoy the presence of God. It is what Exodus is all about: 'I bore you on eagles' wings and brought you to Myself' (Ex. 19:4). It is indeed what Jesus is all about, who died 'the just for the unjust, that He might bring us to God' (1 Pet. 3:18).

REFLECTION

Rejoice that the people of God have 'washed their robes and made them white in the blood of the Lamb. Therefore they are before the throne of God ...' (Rev. 7:14–15).

REFERENCES

1 Frances Havergal, *'Take my life'.*

2 Robert Robinson, *'Come thou fount of every blessing'.*

3 William Cowper, *'There is a fountain filled with blood'.*

4 Johnson Oatman, *'O, pilgrim bound for the heavenly land'.*

5 Fanny Crosby, *'To God be the glory'.*

6 John Newton, *'Glorious things of thee are spoken'.*

7 James Wallace, *'There is an eye that never sleeps'.*

8 John Cowper, *'There is a fountain filled with blood'.*

9 John Newton, *'Approach, my soul, the mercy seat'.*

10 CSM chorus, *'There's a way back to God'.*

11 Isaac Watts, *'Not all the blood of beasts'.*

12 Fanny Crosby, *'Jesus, keep me near the cross'.*

13 Fanny Crosby, *'In truth and grace I want to grow'.*

14 John Newton, *'Glorious things of thee are spoken'.*

Alec Motyer
EXODUS
THE LORD AND HIS PILGRIMS
40 UNDATED DEVOTIONS THROUGH THE BOOK OF EXODUS